CONTENTS

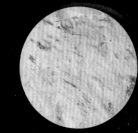

INTRODUCTION

This book is packed full of everything you will need to fire the imagination of a little budding astronaut. The 15 exciting craft projects will allow you and your child to create a whole range of space-themed accessories, toys, and decorations, from padded space boots and an astronaut's helmet, to a shiny rocket pencil case and a constellation night light. Your would-be space explorer can put on a theater show using the friendly astronaut and alien puppets, or blast off into outer space in a giant cardboard rocket.

When all the crafting is done, we show you how to throw the ultimate, out-of-this-world space party, where you get to make use of all your creations. There are ideas for party games, nibbles, and decorations, as well as a recipe for a delicious moon cake, with hidden moon rock in the middle!

The 15 projects vary in terms of length of time required, but all have been designed for those with little crafting experience and can be made by adults with their children. Each project comes with clear, illustrated step-by-step instructions. Templates, when required, can be found at the back of the book (see pages 62–3).

Crafting with kids can be messy, rewarding, hard work, fun, and at times a total disaster! Kids are unpredictable, and we find that it's best to approach any crafting activity with an open mind. Treat the projects in this book as a guide, and use whatever materials you have to hand rather than following the instructions precisely. Put your child's own flair and decoration into each item you are making so that it feels personal to them—if they want a wonky, neon-pink astronaut's helmet covered in glitter then go with it!

We began our blog, Little Button Diaries, as a way of documenting the things we were making for and with our kids. It has evolved and changed as our kids have grown into little (very messy) makers themselves. Our kids are our guinea pigs—everything we make is tried and tested on them. If they don't like it, it doesn't make the cut!

We hope you like our book as much as we enjoyed making it. Happy space crafting!

TOOLS AND MATERIALS

This section provides an overview of the basic craft supplies and materials you will need for the projects within this book. We have tried to ensure that the materials used throughout are inexpensive and readily available, and, where possible, we have used supplies you probably already have in your home.

Art and craft supplies

Paint and brushes
Throughout the book we have used acrylic paint on projects as it gives a thicker and more durable finish, but ready-mixed poster paint is a good child-friendly alternative. For an even coverage, apply several coats. Paintbrushes in a variety of sizes are also helpful.

Glue
White PVA glue is fantastic for children—it's inexpensive, and can be mixed with water to create papier-mâché paste. Glue guns are also invaluable, because the glue dries incredibly quickly and holds very well. Glue guns should obviously only be handled by an adult as they get very hot.

Double-sided tape
We swear by this for mess-free crafting with kids. It instantly sticks together card, paper, and felt, and you can buy strong-sticking varieties too, making it a good (and more child-friendly) alternative to superglue.

Other tapes
Masking tape is fantastic for holding projects together while the glue dries, and it can also be used to create a relief effect with paint. Duct tape is wonderfully versatile, too. It is super-strong, waterproof, and comes in a variety of colors and widths.

Craft foam
This is a fantastic crafting alternative to cardboard or fabric—it's cheap, easy to cut, waterproof, and can even be sewn onto things.

Polymer clay
This is a malleable clay that is baked in the oven. It's great for children because it's brightly colored and really easy to shape. We prefer to use the soft type as it's much easier to work. It is available in craft stores and online.

Other essentials
- Colored permanent marker pens
- Colored card
- Scissors
- Paper plates
- Shrink plastic

Sewing supplies
Three of the projects in this book involve sewing. They can be sewn by hand, but a sewing machine will be much quicker. Whether hand or machine sewing, you will need a selection of colored sewing threads, pins, needles, fabric scissors, and embroidery thread.

Fabrics
Fabrics such as felt, fleece, jersey, and fake leather are great to sew with because the edges don't fray, so you won't need to sew any seams! Felt is particularly good for kids as it is cheap, readily available, comes in bright colors, and can be easily cut, stitched, and glued.

Recycled materials
It's useful to keep a box of things that you would normally throw away, such as cardboard, yogurt pots, plastic bottles, and lids of all shapes and sizes. We raided our recycling bins for most of the projects in this book. Kids love a box of junk to rummage through before getting crafty!

SPACE BOOTS

These boots are made for (moon) walking! They're really simple to put together, too. All you need is an old pair of wellies, duct tape, and some upholstery foam, which you can pick up from a fabric or reupholstery store.

You will need

 Old pair of wellington boots

 Approx 36 x 12in (90 x 30cm) of ½in (1cm)-thick upholstery foam

 White and black duct tape

 Scissors

 Scraps of blue and silver craft foam

 Strong glue

 Planet and planet ring templates, found on page 63

Step 1

First, you need to cover the boots with the upholstery foam, to create a padded effect. Start with the leg of the boot. Wrap the foam around it, cut to size, and tape in place using the white duct tape. Wrap another piece of foam around the toe, cut to size, and secure with tape under the sole of the boot.

Step 2

Wrap a final narrow piece of foam around the heel of the boot, and trim so that it fills the gaps (it's quite squishy so don't worry about being exact). Tape in place.

Step 3

Cover the boot all over with white duct tape. Starting with the leg, work down the length of the boot, wrapping the top of the tape over the rim and under the sole.

Step 4

Next, cover the toe of the boot. This is a bit trickier, because of the bends and curves, but you can avoid creases by snipping into the duct tape to form tabs. When the toe is covered, run tape down the front of the boot to finish.

Step 5

Cover the sole with black duct tape, making sure that the tape extends 1in (2.5cm) up the sides of the boot. Wrap short strips of black duct tape around the rim of the boot too, so that the top of the boot has a 1in (2.5cm) thick black border. Repeat steps 1 to 5 for the second boot.

Step 6

Photocopy the planet and planet ring templates on page 63 and cut them out. Use them to cut out a planet from the silver foam and a ring from the blue foam. Use strong glue to attach them onto the outer side of one of the boots.

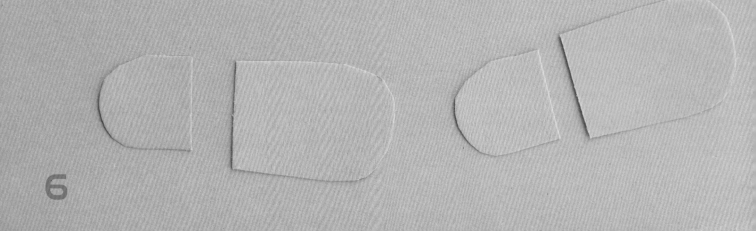

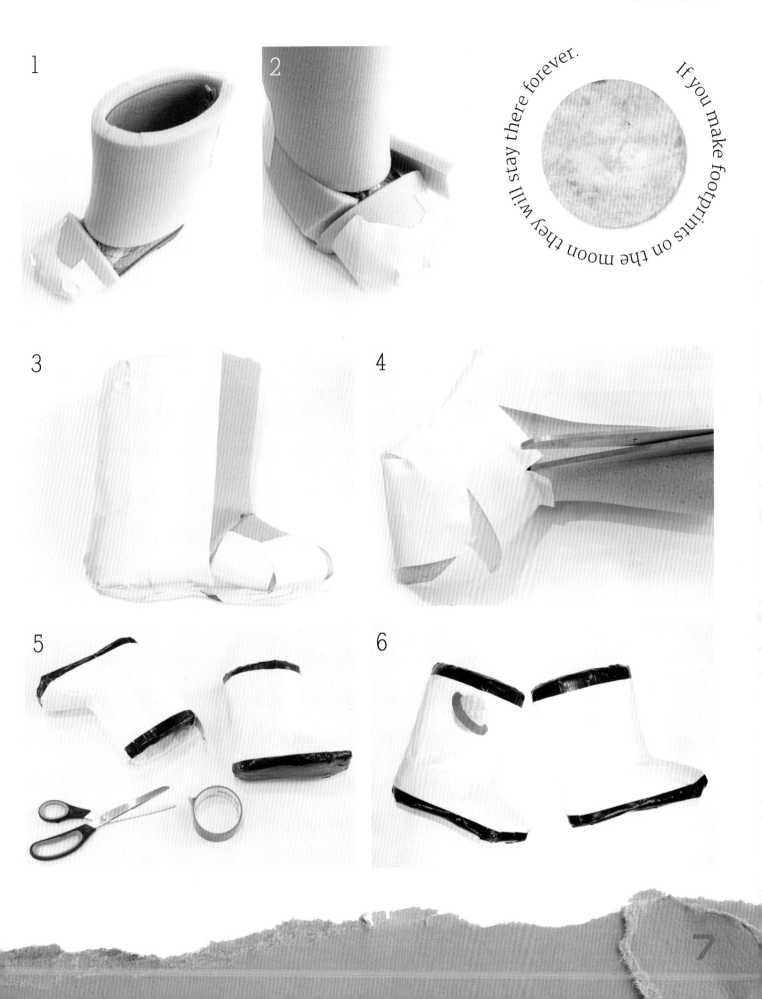

1

2

If you make footprints on the moon they will stay there forever.

3

4

5

6

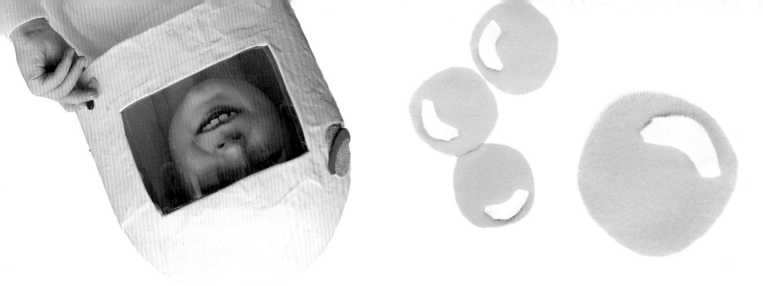

ASTRONAUT'S HELMET

No astronaut's outfit is complete without a helmet, and this one is really easy and fun to make, using a balloon and a little papier-mâché—kids will love getting their hands sticky covering the helmet in gooey newspaper. Note that you will need to apply a few layers of papier-mâché to make the helmet strong—each layer must be dry before the next layer is added, so you will need plenty of patience!

You will need

 Balloon

 Card measuring roughly 6 x 34in (15 x 86cm); you can join together the sides of a cereal box to make one long strip

 Masking tape

 Newspaper

 PVA glue and water

 Paintbrush

 Scissors

 White acrylic paint

 White duct tape

 1 x sheet of acetate measuring 7 x 5in (18 x 13cm)

 Strong glue

 Scraps of blue and silver craft foam

 2 x buttons

 Planet and planet ring templates, found on page 63

8

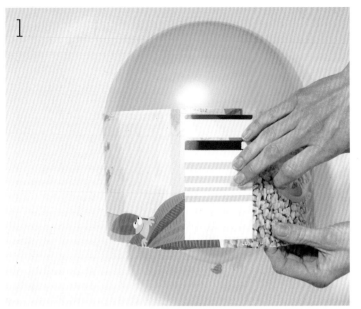

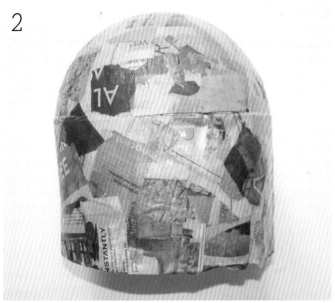

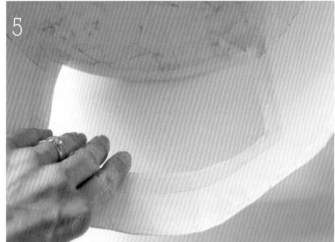

6

Step 1

Blow up your balloon to an approximate diameter of 10in (25cm). Wrap the piece of card snugly around it, and tape the two ends of the card together with masking tape.

Step 2

The card and the top of the balloon can now be covered with papier-mâché. Tear sheets of newspaper into small pieces. Mix up the papier-mâché paste using two parts PVA glue to one part water. Working in sections, use the paintbrush to spread a layer of glue onto the card and balloon, attach the newspaper pieces, then cover with another layer of glue. Once the whole thing is covered, leave to dry overnight. Repeat the process two or three times—more layers will create a stronger helmet. When the final layer is dry, pop the balloon and remove it from the helmet.

Step 3

To create the visor, draw a 6 x 4in (15 x 10cm) rectangle about 2½in (6cm) from the bottom of the helmet, and cut it out.

Step 4

Paint the outside and inside of the helmet white. To give the helmet neater edges, cut small strips of white duct tape and attach them around the bottom of the helmet. Make snips into the tape to form tabs and fold the tabs under the rim. Do the same thing around the visor, but cut the duct tape in half (lengthways) first to make it thinner.

Step 5

Glue the acetate inside the helmet so that it covers the face hole.

Step 6

Photocopy the planet and planet ring templates on page 63 and cut them out. Use them to cut out a planet from the silver foam and a ring from the blue foam. Use strong glue to attach them onto the side of the helmet. Glue two buttons to the other side of the helmet, near the bottom.

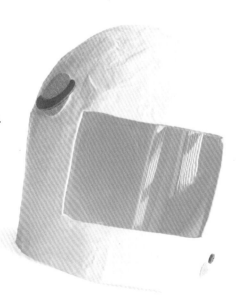

WALKIE TALKIES

Ground Control calling! These walkie talkies are a great way for mini astronauts to keep in contact while in space. You can make them from any small cardboard boxes, but cereal selection boxes work well. The dials and knobs on the walkie talkies can be created using lids and other scraps from the recycling bin. The instructions here are for two walkie talkies, but you can make as many as you need.

You will need

 3 x small rectangular cardboard boxes, e.g. small cereal selection boxes

 Scissors

 Masking tape

 Black, white, and silver duct tape

 2 x jam-jar lids

 Black permanent pen

 Strong glue

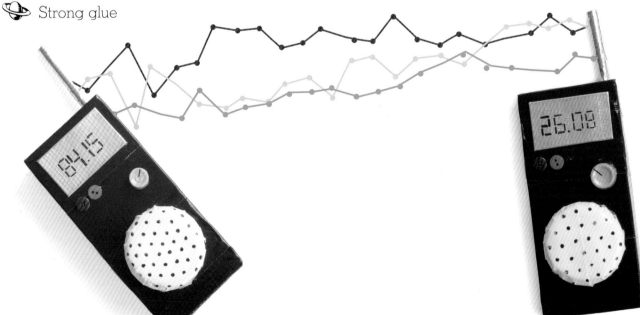 2 x scraps of card, each measuring 2½ x 1½in (6 x 4cm)

Plastic drinking straw

2 x small bottle lids

4 x small buttons

1

2

3

Step 1

Cut one of the cardboard boxes in half widthways. Take one of the halves and, using masking tape, attach it to the end of a second, uncut box to make a longer box. Repeat for the other box.

Step 2

Cover the ends of the boxes with black duct tape. Snip the corners and fold the excess tape neatly down the sides. Then wrap strips of black duct tape widthways around the boxes so that they are completely covered.

Step 3

To create the speakers, take the two jam-jar lids and cover them with white duct tape. Cut tabs in the excess tape and fold over the edges.

Step 4

Using a black permanent pen, draw black dots on the front of the jam-jar lids. Use strong glue to attach the lids onto the walkie talkies, near the bottom.

Step 5

To create the walkie-talkie screen, wrap a 2½ x 1½in (6 x 4cm) rectangle of card in silver duct tape. Add digital numbers using a black permanent pen, and glue to the top of the walkie talkie.

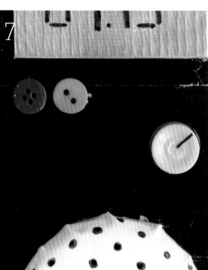

Step 6

To make the aerials, cut a drinking straw into 2½in (6cm) pieces and cover with silver duct tape. Glue onto the top of each walkie talkie, in the corner.

Step 7

Take the two small bottle lids, and draw a line on each of them so that they resemble a dial. Use strong glue to stick the dials onto the walkie-talkies. Attach two small buttons to each walkie-talkie underneath the screen.

15

ALIEN OUTFIT

This colorful, one-size-fits-all alien outfit is like nothing you've seen on Earth. It comes with plenty of wiggly tentacles and three bendy antennae eyes which can peer in different directions at the same time! Fleece is a great fabric for beginner sewers because it doesn't fray, so the raw edges don't need to be neatened. Finish off the outfit with brightly colored trousers, leggings, or tights for an eye-popping extraterrestrial effect.

You will need

For the Tunic:

-  Green fleece measuring about 30 x 60in (80 x 150cm)
- Small side plate
- Fabric scissors
- Tailor's chalk
- Pins
- Sewing machine and matching thread
- 100g ball of blue wool
- 10in (25cm) length each of blue and pink jersey fabric

For the Headband:

- 3 x table tennis balls
- Blue and black permanent markers
- Pin
- Sharp scissors
- 3 x pipe cleaners
- Strong glue
- 2 x sheets of green felt, each measuring about 12 x 8in (30 x 20cm)
- Plastic hairband

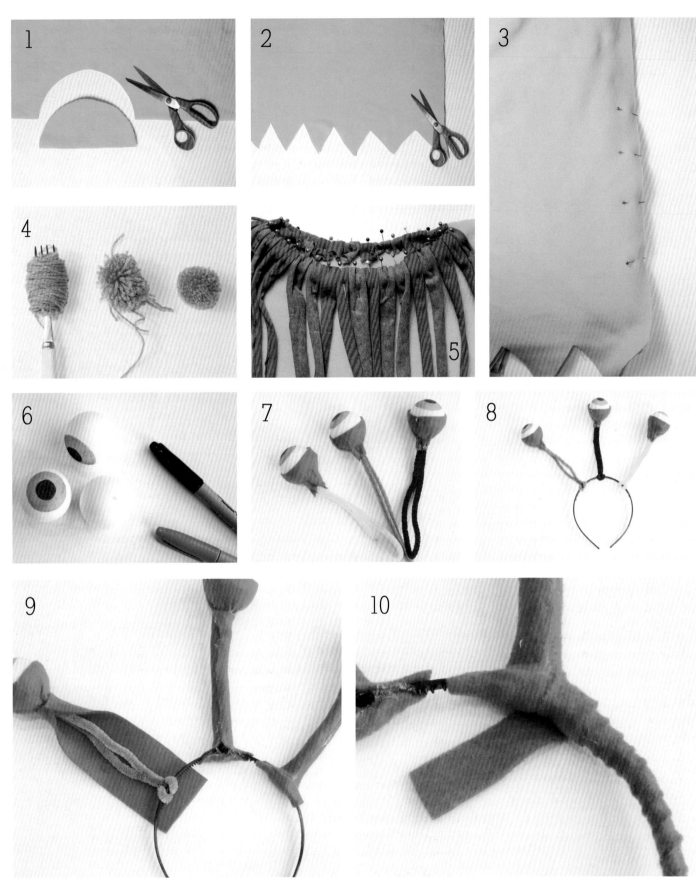

Step 1

To make the tunic neckline, fold the fleece in half widthways and place a side plate in the center across the foldline. Draw around the plate in tailor's chalk, and cut out.

Step 2

Cut a large zig-zag pattern along the bottom of the fabric, with each zig-zag about 4in (10cm) across.

Step 3

Measure halfway up each side of the fabric. Pin and sew the bottom half of the fabric, leaving the top half unsewn to form two armholes. Turn the fabric inside out so that the seams are on the inside.

Step 4

Using the method described in the box opposite, make a batch of blue pom-poms, wrapping the wool around a fork approximately 100 times for each one. We made 20 pom-poms — one for each point on the bottom of the outfit. Hand sew the pom-poms in place along the bottom of the fabric at the end of each zig-zag point.

Step 5

Cut 1in (2.5cm)-wide strips of the blue and pink jersey fabric to different lengths, and pin them around the collar, with 1in (2.5cm) of each strip tucked on the inside of the tunic. Sew in place using a sewing machine.

Step 6

To make the eyes for the headband, draw a blue circle onto each of the table tennis balls, about 1in (2.5cm) wide. Add a smaller black circle in the center for the pupil. Use a pin and some sharp scissors to poke a small hole in the back of the balls.

Step 7

Fold the pipe cleaners in half and insert the ends into the holes in each ball, then glue in place. Cut a square of green felt wide enough to fit around the circumference of the ball. Add glue to the edges of the square and wrap it around the ball, about ½in (1cm) from the eyes. Glue the felt around the rest of the ball and trim the excess. Repeat for the other eyes.

Step 8

Attach the antennae to the hairband by pulling each eye through the loop in the pipe cleaner, in a luggage-label (cow hitch) style knot. Space them equally along the top of the hairband.

Step 9

Cut strips of green felt wide enough to wrap around the pipe cleaners, and a little longer. Glue them around the base of the eye, covering the raw edges of the felt. Then glue the felt all around the pipe cleaners, and fold up the bottom to cover the hairband.

Step 10

To finish the headband, cut 1in (2.5cm)-wide strips of felt. Add glue all the way along and wrap the felt around the whole hairband.

How to make a pom-pom

To make a plain pom-pom, wind the wool around your hand (or a book or fork) a number of times; winding the wool around four fingers 50–60 times will make a pom-pom of about 1½in (4cm). Peel away and tie with another bit of wool in the middle, as tightly as you can. Snip through all the loops and trim the wool to the size you want it.

ROCKET PACK

This rocket pack is the coolest space accessory an astronaut can own. It's easily made from plastic bottles, and comes with flaming boosters and a fuel gauge to make sure you don't run out of gas while flying through the galaxy. The nylon straps are available to buy in craft stores and online, but they're not essential—if you can't find them, just use wide cotton tape or ribbon.

You will need

 2 x 2-liter plastic bottles, empty and with labels and lids removed

 Newspaper

 PVA glue and water

 Paintbrush

 Strong glue

 Red and white acrylic paint

 2 x paper cups

 Scissors

 70in (180cm)-long nylon strap and 2 x sets of buckles

 1 x sheet each of red, orange, and blue felt, measuring 12 x 8in (30 x 20cm)

 Plastic drinking straw

 Masking tape

 Black permanent pen

 Scraps of blue and silver craft foam

 Planet and planet ring templates, found on page 63

The moon is very hot during the day but very cold at night.

1

2

Step 1

Tear the newspaper into small pieces. Make a papier-mâché paste by mixing two parts PVA glue to one part water. Working in sections, use the paintbrush to spread a layer of glue onto the bottle, attach the newspaper pieces, then cover with another layer of glue. Cover both bottles completely with newspaper and leave to dry.

Step 2

Once dry, line up the two bottles lengthways, and use strong glue to stick them together. Once the glue is dry, paint both bottles red.

Step 3

To create the boosters, cut out the base of the paper cups and paint the cups red, inside and out. Once they are dry, glue them onto the lid end of each bottle.

Step 4

Cut the length of nylon strap in half to create two pieces, each measuring 35in (90cm). Thread a buckle onto each end of both straps, then fold over the ends of the straps by 1½in (4cm) and glue to secure in place.

Step 5

Use strong glue to attach the straps along the length of each bottle, with the buckles lined up in the center.

Step 6

To make the flames, cut two strips of 4in (10cm)-wide red felt to fit inside the rim of the paper cups, then cut into the strips to create flame shapes. Repeat with the yellow and blue felt, but cut each pair slightly narrower to get a layered effect.

Step 7

For each set of flames, glue the three layers of felt together, then attach them to the inside rims of the paper cups, using strong glue.

Step 8

To make the fuel indicator, cut a 3in (8cm) piece of plastic drinking straw. Wrap masking tape around the middle of the straw and paint the other half white. Once dry, remove the tape and use a permanent pen to add lines all along the straw. Cut out a rectangle of blue craft foam slightly larger than the straw, and glue the straw in the center. Then attach the fuel indicator to the rocket pack using strong glue.

Step 9

Photocopy the planet and planet ring templates on page 63 and cut them out. Use them to cut out a planet from the blue foam and a ring from the silver foam. Use strong glue to attach them to the rocket pack top.

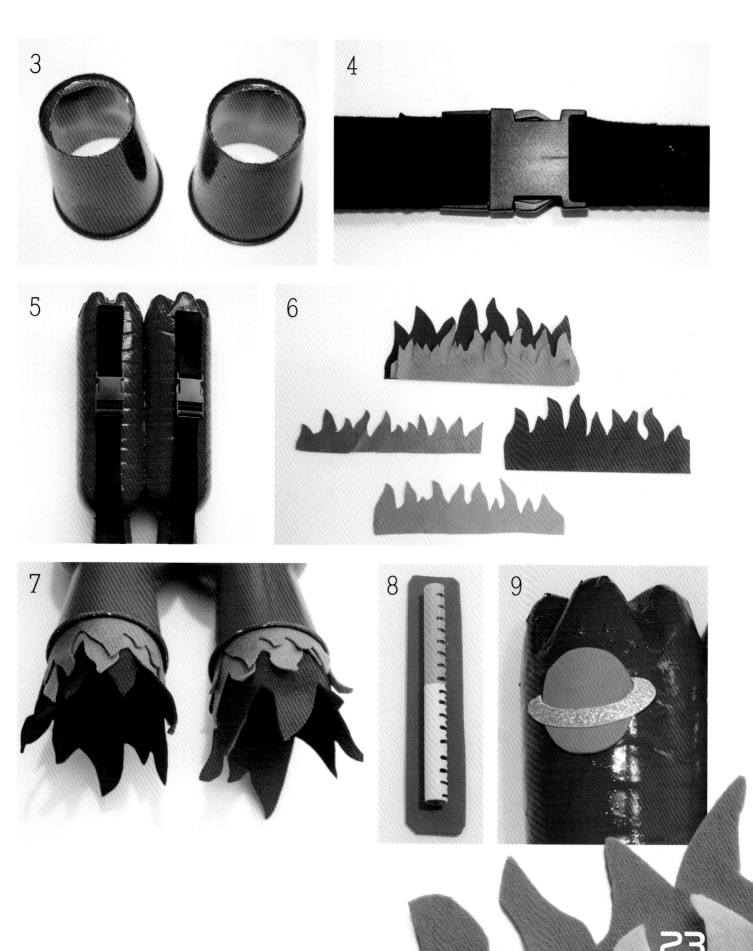

TOY UFO AND ROCKET

This kids' craft activity is a fab way to keep little astronauts busy between missions. Both the rocket and the UFO are painted using glow-in-the-dark paint, which you can buy online or from large craft stores. The rocket comes complete with a little polymer clay astronaut, while the UFO has a friendly green alien.

You will need

For the UFO:

 2 x paper bowls

 Strong glue

 Clear yogurt pot, empty and with labels removed

 Pencil

 Glow-in-the-dark paint in two colors

 Paintbrush

 Decorative tape

 Small lumps of polymer clay in green, white, black, and red

 Permanent coloring pens

For the Rocket:

 500ml plastic bottle, empty and with labels and lids removed

 Scissors

 Scrap of red card

 Masking tape

 Corrugated card

 Strong glue

 Newspaper

 PVA glue and water

 Glow-in-the-dark paint in two colors

 Paintbrush

 Silver acrylic paint

 Silver craft foam

 Small lumps of polymer clay in silver, pale pink, and red

 Permanent blue and red pens

 Rocket feet template, found on page 62

24

UFO

Step 1

Glue the paper bowls together to form a UFO shape. If your bowls are quite thin, you can strengthen them by gluing pairs together before you start.

Step 2

Place the yogurt pot upside down in the center of the UFO and draw around it in pencil. Remove the pot and paint the UFO with glow-in-the-dark paint, painting the circle in a contrasting color. Once dry, add decorative tape around the edge of the bowls for a neater finish.

Step 3

To make the alien, roll a cherry-size lump of green polymer clay into a sausage shape, about 1½in (4cm) long. Roll two small horns and a tail from the green clay and press them firmly onto the body. Roll a tiny ball of white clay, squash it flat, and place it on the front of the alien for an eye, then add a dot of black clay for the pupil. Use the back of a teaspoon handle to push a mouth shape into the clay and add a small sausage of red inside for a tongue. Bake in the oven according to the manufacturer's instructions.

Step 4

Draw spots for lights around the rim of the yogurt pot using permanent pens. Glue the alien onto the UFO, inside the circle, and glue the yogurt pot on top.

Rocket

Step 1

Draw a circle around 2in (5cm) in diameter, roughly 2in (5cm) from the bottom of the bottle, and cut it out. Then cut the bottle in half just above the circle.

Step 2

Next, make the astronaut a ledge to stand on. Draw around the cut side of the bottle onto the red card, then draw another circle ½in (1cm) bigger around it, and cut it out. Create tabs in the circle by snipping up to the smaller circle and folding back the card. Tape the ledge inside the top half of the bottle.

Step 3

Stick the two halves of the bottle back together using masking tape, then use the template found on page 62 to cut out three rocket feet from corrugated card. Space them equally around the top of the bottle (which is now the bottom of the rocket!) and attach using strong glue.

Step 4

Tear the newspaper into small pieces. Make a papier-mâché paste by mixing two parts PVA glue to one part water. Working in sections, spread a layer of glue onto the rocket, attach the newspaper pieces, then cover with another layer of glue. Cover the bottle and feet completely with newspaper, and leave to dry overnight.

Step 5

Paint the rocket using glow-in-the-dark paint for the body, and silver for the feet. Use another shade of glow-in-the-dark paint to add a trim to the window and buttons on the front. Cut a 5in (13cm)-diameter circle from silver craft foam, and cut it in half. Fold to create a cone and glue together, using masking tape while it dries if needed. Glue to the top.

Step 6

To make the astronaut's head, roll a small ball of pale pink polymer clay. For the helmet, roll out a small piece of silver, around ⅛in (3mm) thick. Cut one side away to form a straight edge and cut away a small ½in (1cm) square just above the straight line to form the visor. Wrap the helmet carefully onto the head, cut away the excess clay, and smooth down.

Step 7

For the body, roll a thumb-size piece of silver polymer clay into a sausage shape, slightly tapering it at one end. Attach the body to the head. For the rocket pack, roll a small lump of red clay into a sausage shape, about ¼in (6mm) thick, and cut it into two 2in (5cm)-long pieces. Stick together lengthways, then attach to the back of the astronaut. Bake in the oven as per the manufacturer's instructions.

Step 8

Once the astronaut is cool, draw on a face using permanent pen. Glue or place into the ledge in the rocket.

UFO

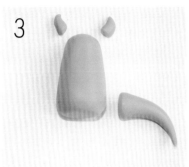

1

2

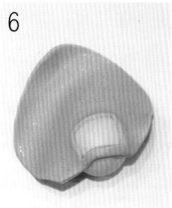

3

4

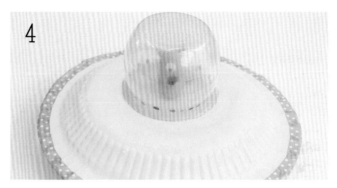

Rocket

1

2

3

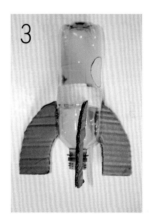

4

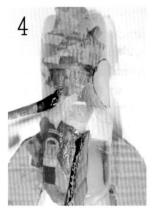

5

6

7

8

CONSTELLATION NIGHT LIGHT

This night light is a great way to teach children about constellations, and it looks lovely twinkling away on a bedroom wall or shelf at night. Before you start, have a look on the Internet and pick a constellation you'd like to feature. We've shown Ursa Major—the Great Bear—but you could personalize your night light by using your child's star sign, or a constellation you can see from your house. It's best to use a glue gun to attach the fairy lights because the glue dries very quickly, but if you don't have one you could use strong glue and masking tape to secure the lights while the glue sets.

You will need

 Large square art canvas, about 20 x 20in (50 x 50cm)

 Navy blue, white, pale blue, and red acrylic paint

 Large paintbrush

 Newspaper

 Battery-operated fairy lights

 Pencil

 Sharp scissors

 Glue gun

Step 1

Paint the canvas navy blue all over, including the sides. You may need two coats to ensure an even coverage. Leave to dry.

Step 2

Place the canvas onto sheets of newspaper on the floor. Mix a blob of white paint with a small amount of water until it is the consistency of thick cream. Dip the paintbrush into the paint then, standing up so that you aren't too close, drip paint drops onto the canvas to create the effect of a starry sky. Repeat with the red and pale blue paint.

Step 3

Choose the constellation you would like to feature, then count the number of fairy lights—check that your constellation has the same number or fewer stars than there are lights! Remember, too, that the lead of the lights will need to stretch between each star. Mark the location of the stars in pencil on the front of the canvas.

Step 4

Use a pair of sharp scissors to poke holes into the front of the canvas at each of the pencil marks. The holes should be just big enough to fit the end of a fairy light through.

Step 5

Poke the first fairy light through one of the holes and glue it in place using a glue gun. Hold the light for a short time until the glue has set. Repeat for the other fairy lights, then tuck any excess lights out of the way and glue the battery pack into one of the corners of the canvas to conceal it.

5

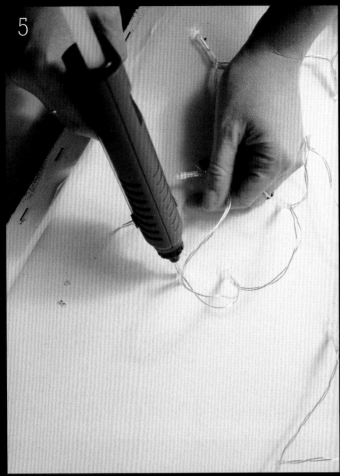

The Milky Way is a spiral-shaped galaxy that contains over 100 billion stars, including our own solar system spinning around our own star, the Sun.

GIANT ROCKET DEN

5... 4... 3... 2... 1... Blast off! What child wouldn't love hiding away in a giant rocket den? All you need to create this fab space shuttle is a few cardboard boxes, some bottle lids, and a bit of duct tape to hold it all together. The supplies listed below are just guidelines—have a rummage through your recycling box and see what you can find that looks as if it might belong on a rocket. You can use whatever size boxes you can find—the bigger the better!

You will need

 3 x large (about 27½in/70cm) square cardboard boxes

 Silver duct tape

 Sharp serrated knife

 Blue paint and silver acrylic spray paint

 Paintbrush

 Selection of jar and bottle lids, including a large lid (e.g., a laundry detergent bottle)

 Glue gun

 A4 sheets of silver, blue, and red craft foam

 Black felt-tip pen

 Small and large dinner plates (or a large compass)

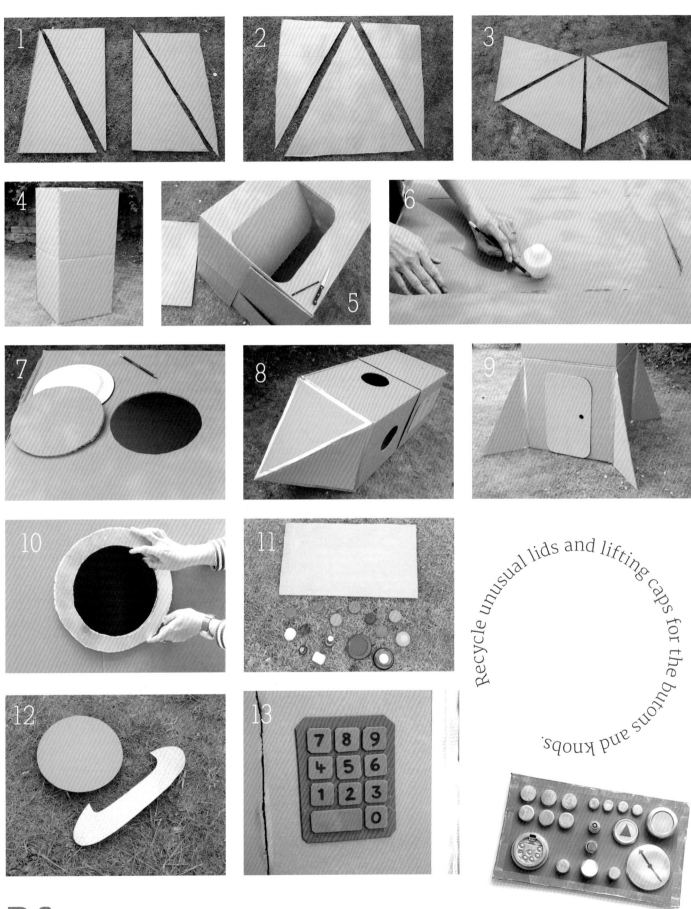

Recycle unusual lids and lifting caps for the buttons and knobs.

Step 1

Begin by cutting off the top flaps from two of the boxes. Take two of the removed flaps and cut in half diagonally to create four rocket feet.

Step 2

Take the third box and cut apart along the folds, removing the flaps, to create four main square panels. To turn these panels into the top pyramid of the rocket, measure halfway along one edge to find the center point on each panel. Then draw a diagonal line from that point to the bottom corners to create a triangle. Cut each one out.

Step 3

Paint the pyramid triangles and feet triangles blue. Paint the feet on both sides and leave to dry.

Step 4

Open the bottom flaps of one of the boxes and insert the box, flaps down, into the top of the other box so that you have one tall open box. They should fit neatly together without having to tape together, but tape using duct tape if necessary.

Step 5

Make the rocket door by drawing a large rectangle (you can draw around one of the removed flaps for this) in the center of the bottom box. Add rounded edges and cut out, leaving a hinge on one of the long sides. Be sure to cut through the flap (from the top box) on the inside, too.

Step 6

Draw around a large detergent bottle lid about halfway down the door for the handle. Cut out the circle using a sharp serrated knife. Paint the door blue on both sides. Spray paint the detergent lid silver and leave to dry.

Step 7

Use a small dinner plate (or a compass) to cut circular windows in three sides of the rocket (leaving the back wall for the control panel) in the top box. Cut out.

Step 8

Use silver duct tape to tape each top triangle onto the open edges of the box. Then tape each one together to form a pyramid at the top of the rocket.

Step 9

Tape the long straight side of the rocket feet onto the bottom corners of the box using a strip of duct tape on the front and back.

Step 10

For the window frames, draw around a bigger dinner plate onto some excess cardboard. Place the original plate in the middle of the cardboard circle and draw around it to form an inner circle. Cut this out then repeat to make two more rings for each window. Spray paint them silver and glue onto the windows.

Step 11

For the control panel cut a rectangle from one of the discarded flaps measuring about 18 x 10in (45 x 25cm). Paint blue and leave to dry. Spray paint a variety of different lids silver. Add a trim of silver tape around the edge of the blue card then use a glue gun to stick the lids on. Glue the control panel into the rocket. You can also paint and attach any other interesting old trays, tubes, and containers for added effect.

Step 12

For the saturn planet symbol, cut a circle from blue foam about 5in (13cm) in diameter. Make a ring to go around it from silver foam, using the width of the blue circle as a template, then cut out. Glue them together onto the top box of the rocket.

Step 13

To make the door's pin pad, cut 10 small buttons about 1in (2.5cm) square from some blue foam. Cut one larger button about 2 x 1in (5 x 2.5cm). Trim the corners slightly then glue the buttons onto a piece of red foam in a grid pattern. Use a black felt-tip pen to add numbers onto the buttons, then glue the pin pad next to the door. Glue the detergent lid into the hole on the door.

SPACE RACE GAME

This space-themed variation on the classic Snakes and Ladders game is a race to see who can make it back to Earth first! Shooting stars and rockets propel you faster up the board, while black holes see you sucked back toward the Moon.

You will need

 1 x sheet of mount board or thick card, measuring 16 x 12in (42 x 30cm)

 Ruler

 Pencil

 Cup and bowl

 Permanent colored pens

 Roll of clear self-adhesive contact paper (sticky back plastic)

 1 x sheet of white shrink film (plastic), measuring 12 x 8in (30 x 20cm)

 A dice

 Astronaut template, found on page 62

1

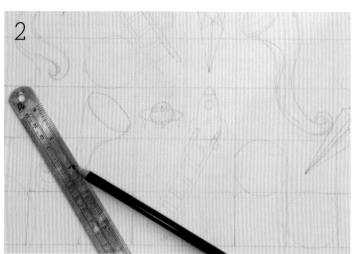

2

3

4

5

6

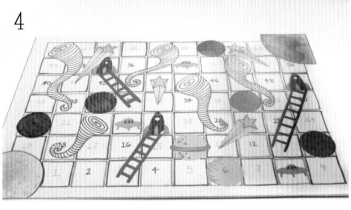

Step 1

Mark a ¾in (2cm)-wide border in pencil around the board, then divide it up into 70 x 1½in (4cm)-wide squares. With the board in landscape, draw around a cup in the bottom left-hand corner to create the Moon. Then draw around a bowl in the top right-hand corner to create a quarter circle for the Earth.

Step 2

Using a pencil, draw on planets, UFOs, shooting stars, black holes, and rockets with boarding ladders. Each planet and UFO should fill a distinct square on the board. Make sure that the tops and bottoms of the shooting stars, black holes, and ladders sit within a square too—as in the classic Snakes and Ladders game.

Step 3

Color in the pictures using bright colored permanent pens, then rub out the pencil marks. Color in the Earth and write 'HOME' in the center. Color in the Moon (pencil works well for this) and add 'START' to the center. Add a border to each square, in alternating colors. Where there is space, add numbers to the squares, starting at the bottom left corner and going up the board. Make sure the numbers snake up the board in a back-and-forth direction so that you can follow them during play.

Step 4

Cover the board in contact paper/ sticky back plastic. Use a ruler to smooth it out, and wrap it around the edges.

Step 5

To make the game pieces, use the astronaut image on page 62 as a guide to draw four (or more if needed) astronauts onto shrink plastic in pencil. You can trace the outline of the image onto paper and cut this out to create a template if you prefer. The astronauts should be about 4in (10cm) tall. Go over the astronaut outline with black permanent pen and rub out the pencil marks.

Step 6

Make each astronaut a different color, using permanent pens. Choose light colors if possible, as the ink will darken when the pieces shrink. If you like, you can personalize the astronauts with your family's initials. Carefully cut them out, then shrink them in the oven, following the manufacturer's instructions. Watch as the pieces curl up and wiggle about—don't remove them until they have fully flattened again.

How to play

Play the game like the classic Snakes and Ladders, rolling the dice to see who can make it all the way up the board first. If you land on a rocket's boarding ladder, climb it. If you land on the tail of a star, shoot up it. Land on a black hole, however, and you'll be sucked back down it. Skip a turn if you land on a UFO, and roll again if you land on a planet. The first one back to Earth wins!

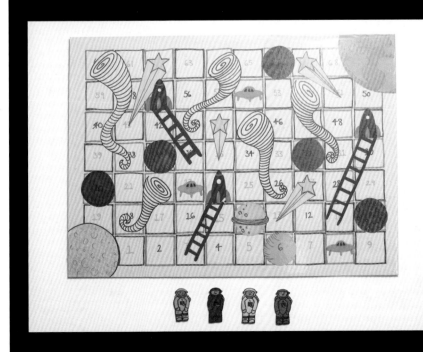

ROCKET PENCIL CASE

This pencil case is the perfect place to store all your important space-tionery! It's made from fake leather, which you can pick up online or from fabric stores. Fake leather is a fantastic material because it's super-sturdy, water-resistant, and doesn't fray. Thick materials like this are best sewn on a machine, which is what we've done here, but if you prefer to sew by hand, try using felt instead.

You will need

 Square of silver fake leather, measuring about 15 x 15in (40 x 40cm)

 One square each of red and black fake leather, measuring about 4 x 4in (10 x 10cm)

 Fabric scissors

 Pins

 Sewing machine with zipper foot, and white thread

 Silver or gray zip at least 5in (13cm) long

 Rocket pencil case templates, found on page 62

41

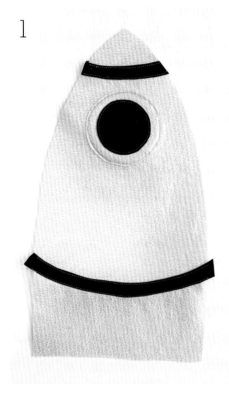

1

Step 1

Photocopy the templates on page 62 and cut them out. Use them to cut out the following: two rockets, one middle booster, four side boosters, and one outer window from the silver fake leather; one inner window, one long strip, and one short strip from the black fake leather; and five flames from the red fake leather. Line up and pin the long and short strips across the width of one of the rocket pieces, at the top and near the base. Pin the outer window under the top strip. Sew all three pieces of leather in place, neatly along the edges. Pin the inner window on top of the outer window and sew along the edge.

Step 2

Pin the middle booster in the center of the rocket, 1½in (4cm) from the bottom. Tuck one of the flames just under the bottom, and sew the booster in place along the edges.

Step 3

Pin and sew the two remaining flames together in pairs, wrong sides facing. Pin them between the two side boosters, poking out of the bottom as before, and sew around the edge of the boosters.

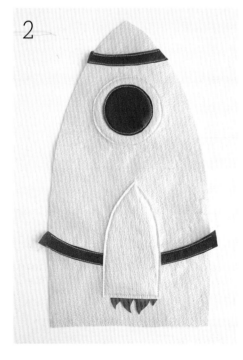

2

3

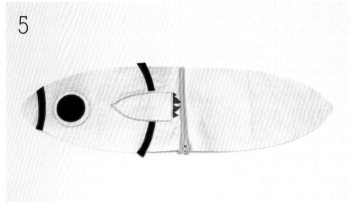

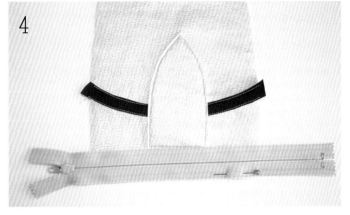

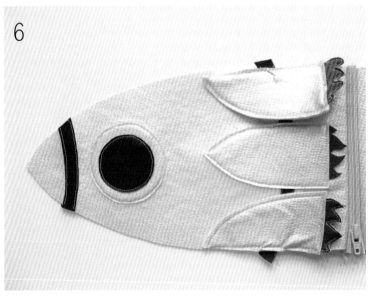

Step 4

Place the zip, right side down, along the bottom of the rocket with the edges lined up. Pin and sew in place using the zipper foot on your sewing machine, close to the zip.

Step 5

Line up the raw edge of the zip with the other rocket piece, right sides together. Pin and sew as before. Slide the zipper into the center and trim the zip to the size of the rocket base, if necessary.

Step 6

Pin the side boosters onto the front of the rocket, with the edges lined up and the bottoms of the boosters at the same level as the central one. Sew along the straight edge only to secure. Open up the zip and pin the rocket right sides together. Sew all the way round with a ¼in (5mm) seam allowance. Turn the right way out.

MISSION CONTROL DESK

This Mission Control Desk provides hours of fun for little flight controllers wanting to manage missions to space. You'll need to collect a heap of bottle tops and lids before you start—we used milk bottle, flip-cap, coffee, and spice jar lids, as well as detergent capsules, but you can use whatever you can find (the more unusual the better!). Bear in mind you will need six matching lids, like the different colored milk bottle lids we've used here, and one large red lid.

You will need

 Piece of white hardboard, measuring 25 x 20in (65 x 50cm)

 Masking tape

 Pencil

 Blue and red acrylic paint

 Paintbrush

 Black chalkboard paint

 8mm-diameter wooden dowel

 Glue gun

 Drill and 8.5mm drill bit

 2 x strips of wood, each measuring 20 x ½in (50 x 1.5cm)

 Small handsaw

 2 x strips of wood, each measuring 14 x ½in (35 x 1.5cm)

 Selection of bottle tops and jar lids

 Permanent pens in a range of colors

 2 x cardboard tubes

 Scissors

 Silver spray paint

 1 x small spring

 A few buttons

 Bulldog clip

 Scrap of black card

 Correction fluid pen

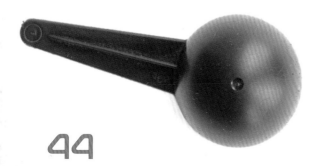

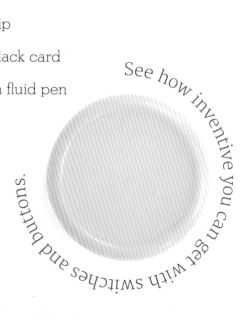

See how inventive you can get with switches and buttons.

Step 1

Place three strips of masking tape diagonally across the bottom left-hand corner of the board. Paint the area in between the tape blue. Once dry, remove the masking tape. Use a cup or bowl to mark a circle in the top left-hand corner of the board in pencil, and add a Saturn ring around it. Paint the planet blue and the ring red.

Step 2

Use a pencil to mark a 9 x 8in (23 x 20cm) rectangle in the center of the board, toward the bottom. Put masking tape outside the lines and paint the rectangle with black chalkboard paint. Remove the masking tape when dry.

Step 3

Cut the dowel into six 1in (2.5cm)-long pieces with the small saw. Add a ring of glue around one end of each dowel, and leave to dry.

Step 4

On the right-hand side of the black rectangle, use a pencil to make six equally spaced marks onto the board, about 4in (10cm) apart. Drill through each of the marks.

Step 5

Flip the board over and glue the four strips of wood, slightly in from the edge, onto the back so that they form a rectangle, avoiding the holes in the board.

Step 6

Select six matching bottle lids in different colors. Insert the pieces of dowel through the back of each hole on the board, with the glued end under the board. Glue a lid onto the top of each piece of dowel in the center. Use permanent pen to mark a line from the center to the edge of each lid, then add shapes, numbers, or letters around each dial.

Step 7

To make the pen pots, cut one third of the length off one of the cardboard tubes, so that you have three tubes of different lengths. Spray the tubes silver. When dry, glue the tubes just above the top left-hand corner of the chalkboard.

Step 8

To make the rocket launch button, glue a spring onto the top of a jar lid, then glue a larger red lid onto the other end of the spring. (If you do not have a red lid you can paint one.) Glue the launch button onto the board in the top right-hand corner. Draw a picture of a rocket underneath, and color in.

Step 9

Spray a selection of lids and bottle tops silver, and glue at various positions onto the board, along with some buttons. Glue the bulldog clip to the top of the chalkboard.

Step 10

Finally, for the countdown clock, cut a rectangle of black card measuring about 4 x 1½in (10 x 4cm). Add the digital numbers using a fluid correction pen, and glue above the chalkboard.

The buttons and knobs are best spray-painted for an even coverage. This should be done by an adult in a well-ventilated area.

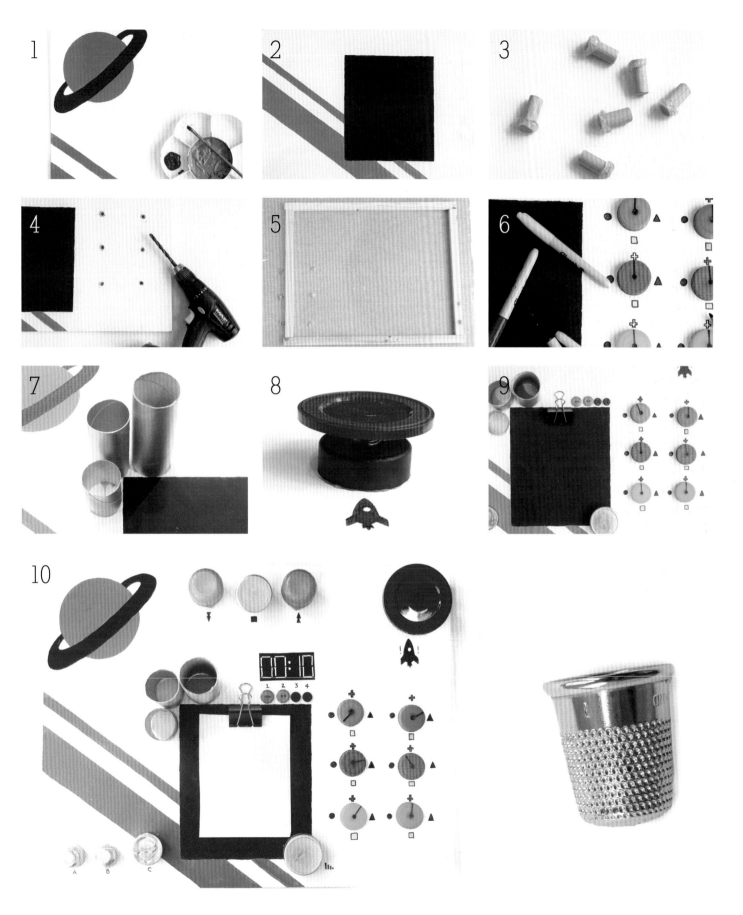

SOLAR SYSTEM MOBILE

This pom-pom space mobile not only looks beautiful, but is also a great way to teach children about the planets in our solar system. It is made up of ten pom-poms, including a giant Sun in the center, a ringed Saturn, and of course our own planet Earth, complete with a teeny tiny Moon.

You will need

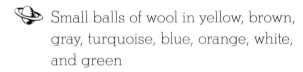 Small balls of wool in yellow, brown, gray, turquoise, blue, orange, white, and green

Small book measuring roughly 5 x 8in (13 x 20cm)

Fork

Scissors

1 x sheet of gray felt measuring roughly 8 x 5in (20 x 13cm)

Craft/PVA glue

Large embroidery hoop, 8in (20cm) in diameter

Small embroidery hoop, 4in (10cm) in diameter

Silver acrylic paint and paintbrush

Nylon thread

How to make your planet pom-poms

To make	Colors required	Wrap around	How many times (roughly)	Pom-pom style
The Sun	Yellow	Width of small book	250	Plain
Jupiter	Brown & gray	Width of small book	160	Patched
Saturn	Yellow & gray	4 fingers	120	Speckled
Uranus	Turquoise	4 fingers	100	Plain
Neptune	Blue	4 fingers	100	Plain
Venus	Orange	3 fingers	100	Plain
Earth	White, blue, & green	Fork	60	Patched
Mars	Orange & brown	Fork	40	Speckled
Mercury	Gray	Fork	30	Plain
Moon	Gray	Fork	20	Plain

1

Step 1

Make each of the planets, the Sun, and the Moon, using the table above. To make plain pom-poms, see page 19 and to make the speckled and patched pom-poms, see the box opposite.

Speckled pom-poms

Take two (or more) strands of different colors and wind them together.

Patched pom-poms

Wind the wool about ten times using one color, then swap to another color and wind another ten times, then repeat.

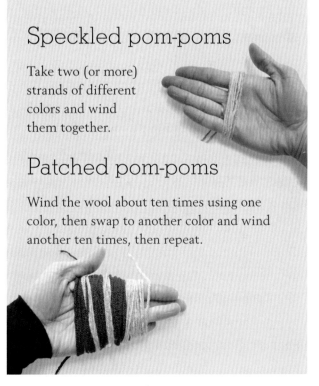

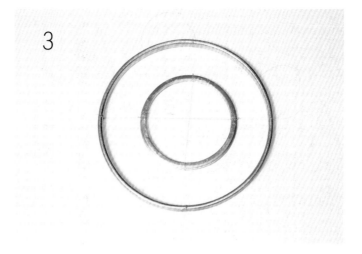

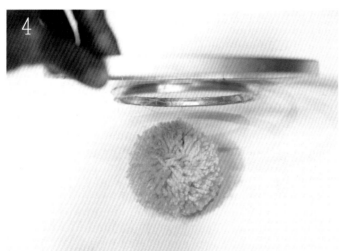

Step 2

To make Saturn's ring, draw around a glass onto the gray felt, then draw another smaller circle in the center, using an egg cup or something of a similar size. Cut out the inner ring. Make a second ring in the same way, and glue the two rings together. Once dry, slip onto the middle of the Saturn pom-pom.

Step 3

Paint both of the embroidery hoops silver. Once dry, use four lengths of nylon thread to tie the smaller hoop into the middle of the larger one. In the middle hoop, tie two lengths of thread to form a cross in the middle.

Step 4

Tie a 10in (25cm) length of nylon thread around the Sun and attach it to the middle of the thread cross in the inner hoop.

Step 5

Now add the planets. Each hoop will have four planets attached. Working down from the planet nearest the Sun, tie the first planet (Mercury) onto the inner hoop, hanging a little lower than the Sun. Add the next three planets (Venus, Earth, Mars) to the inner hoop, each time hanging the planets a little lower than the previous one. Hang the final four planets (Jupiter, Saturn, Uranus, and Neptune) on the outer hoop in the same way. Attach the Moon to the Earth, so that it hangs a couple of inches below it.

Use this easy mnemonic for remembering the order of the planets: 'My Very Educated Mother Just Served Us Noodles.'

ASTRONAUT AND ALIEN HAND PUPPETS

Your little space explorers can put on a cosmic show with these astronaut and alien felt hand puppets. They're easy to make using a sewing machine, but could be sewn by hand with a little time and patience. For a neat finish, sew about ⅛in (2–3mm) from the edge of the felt unless otherwise stated.

You will need

 Fabric scissors

 Pins

 Sewing machine or sewing needle, and matching thread

 Templates, found on pages 62–3

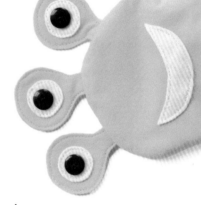

For the Alien:

 2 x squares of bright green felt, each measuring 12 x 12in (30 x 30cm)

 1 square each of blue and white felt, each measuring 4 x 4in (10 x 10cm)

 3 x ½in (1cm)-diameter black buttons

For the Astronaut:

 2 x squares of white felt, each measuring 12 x 12in (30 x 30cm)

 Strip of black felt measuring 5 x ½in (13 x 1cm)

 Square of pink felt measuring 6 x 6in (15 x 15cm)

 Pencil

 Black, red, blue, and yellow embroidery thread

 Embroidery needle

Alien

Step 1

Photocopy the templates on pages 62–3 and cut them out. Use them to cut out two body pieces and six antennae from the green felt; three eyes and a smile from the white felt; and a tummy piece from the blue felt.

Step 2

To make three antennae, pin and sew the white circles onto the center of the green antennae, then stitch a black button into the middle of each. Pin another green antenna onto the back and sew together.

Step 3

Pin the tummy piece onto one of the body pieces, lining up the bottom edges. Pin the smile onto the face and sew both in place. Use blue thread for the tummy and white for the smile.

Step 4

Place the antennae onto the front body piece, right sides together, with the antennae pointing downward and with their bottom edges lined up with the top edge of the head. Position one in the center and the other two 1in (2.5cm) to either side, then pin to secure.

Step 5

Pin the two body pieces right sides together, with the antennae inside. Sew around the puppet from one corner to the other with a ¼in (5mm) seam allowance. Make snips into the curves. Turn the right way out.

Astronaut

Step 1

Use the templates on page 63 to cut out the following: a body piece, a helmet, and a tummy piece from the white felt; a face from the pink felt; and a belt from the black felt.

Step 2

Pin the bottom of the pink face piece to the top of the tummy piece, with a ¼in (5mm) overlap (tummy piece on top), then sew together.

Step 3

Line up the edges and pin and sew the helmet on top of the face, leaving the bottom of the helmet unsewn. Use a pencil to mark two eyes and a mouth onto the face, then use embroidery thread to back stitch a red mouth and black eyes (see box).

Step 4

Pin and sew the belt in place, using the template as a guide. Add a few decorative stitches to the center of the belt using embroidery thread. For the Saturn emblem, stitch a small blue circle on the body about 2in (5cm) from the edge. Fill in the circle using satin stitch, and add a little yellow ring using back stitch.

Step 5

Pin the two body pieces right sides together and sew around the puppet from one corner to the other with a ¼in (5mm) seam allowance. Make snips into the curves. Turn the right way out.

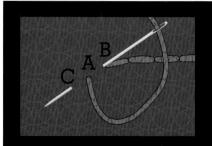

Back stitch

Using the illustration as a guide, bring the needle up through the back of the fabric at A, about ⅛in (3mm) along the line you want to stitch. Push the needle back down at B. Bring the needle up again at C, and then down again at A. Work along like this to create a neat continuous line.

Satin stitch

Begin by back-stitching around the outline of the shape. To fill it, bring the needle in through the fabric from the back, through the stitched outline. Bring the needle across to the other side of the shape, then through the stitched outline as before. Come back through the fabric alongside your original stitch. Continue to fill the whole shape.

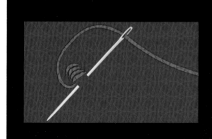

Alien

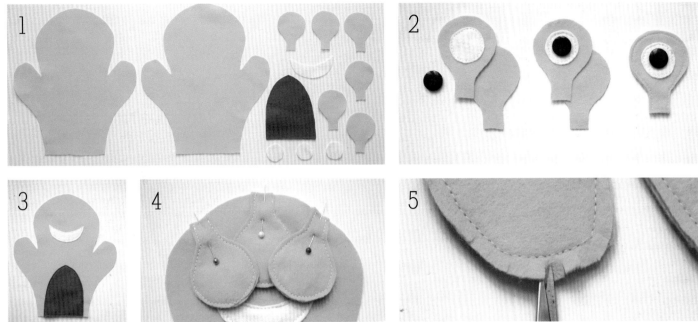

Astronaut

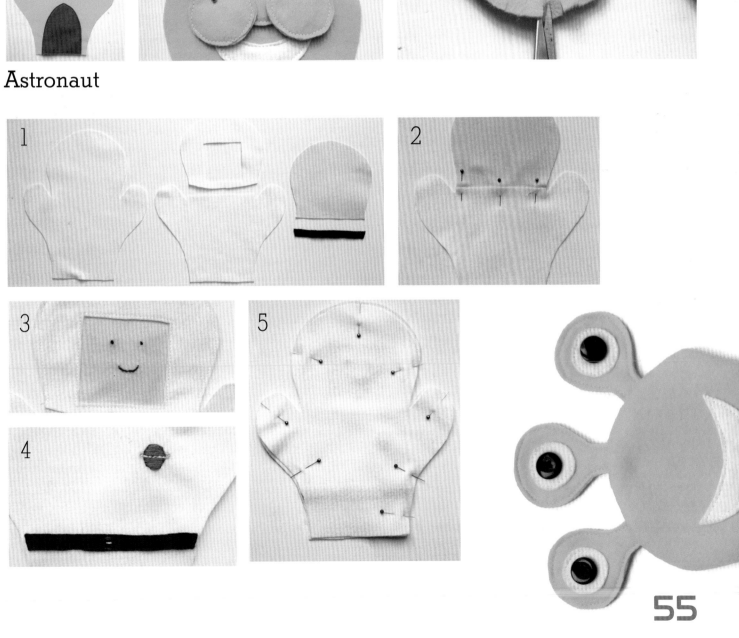

SPACE PARTY

Little astronauts need a party that is out of this world! This section will provide you with top tips for throwing the perfect space party, with loads of ideas for space-tacular food, games, and decorations.

Party Nibbles

Space-themed party food is easy to create. Use rocket or star-shaped cookie cutters to cut sandwiches and cheese straws into space shapes. To make a moon cake, see page 58.

UFO cupcakes

Decorate cupcakes with green frosting and use a dab of frosting to stick an edible eye onto a sweet. Place the sweet in the center of the cake and cover with a clear plastic shot glass. Decorate the cupcakes with colored sugar sweets around the edge to look like a UFO.

Space jelly

Create alien jelly using green jelly (or Jell-O) decorated with edible eyes, or galaxy jelly—blue jelly darkened with food coloring and sprinkled with edible stars and glitter.

Fruit rockets

Cut a small trianglar wedge of watermelon, then thread onto a wooden skewer, followed by banana slices, grapes, and a strawberry.

Peach planets

Sprinkle some donut peaches with glitter and edible stars.

Drinks

Fill a decanter with red juice and label it "Rocket Fuel," or add a few drops of blue food coloring to orange juice to create a delightfully green "Alien Juice."

Decorations

Giant cardboard rocket

See page 32 for details of how to create the centerpiece for your party—a giant rocket den! The Mission Control Desk (see page 44) will allow mini-astronauts to launch each other into space.

Glow-in-the-dark decorations

Decorate the room with glow-in-the-dark stars, add glow sticks to balloons, and paint cardboard cutouts of rockets, aliens, and astronauts using glow-in-the-dark paint. Give each child a glow stick and switch out the lights! Add a UV light for extra luminance.

Table decorations

Take a navy tablecloth and sprinkle on pom-pom planets (see page 48), stars, glitter, and toy aliens.

Games & Activities

Catch a star

Cut gold stars from card, and stick to walls and other objects throughout your house and garden. Then go on a star-catching adventure to see who can collect the most.

Pin the rocket on the moon

Cut out and decorate a large circle of card to resemble the moon, and mark on an "X" for the landing pad. Cut a batch of simple cardboard rocket silhouettes—prelabeled with each child's name—and allow children to decorate them, then add a little blu-tack to the back of each one. Blindfold the children and see who can land their rocket nearest to the moon landing pad.

Black hole star toss

Cut out a large cardboard circle and paint it black, then cut out a selection of small cardboard stars or rockets (labeled for each child). Place the black hole on the floor. Kids can then take it in turns to throw their stars onto the hole from a distance. The star nearest the middle wins.

MOON CAKE

This moon cake is made from the yummiest sponge and has a surprise for little astronauts inside—a cascade of shimmering moon rock! To create the spherical shape, you'll need dome or hemisphere cake tins, or an ovenproof glass bowl.

You will need

For the cake:
- 2 x 8in (20cm) hemisphere cake tins
- 1lb 4oz (550g) softened butter
- 1lb 4oz (550g) caster sugar
- 10 medium eggs
- 20oz (550g) self-rising flour, sifted
- 5 tsp (25g) baking powder
- 1 tsp (5ml) vanilla extract

For the buttercream frosting:
- 9oz (250g) softened butter
- 1lb 5oz (600g) confectioners' (icing) sugar
- 1 tsp (5ml) vanilla extract
- 2 tbsp (30ml) milk
- Black gel food coloring

To decorate:
- 9oz (250g) gray ready-to-roll fondant icing
- 2oz (50g) red ready-to-roll fondant icing
- 2 or 3 different-size (up to 2in/5cm) circular cookie cutters
- Edible silver glitter
- Black gel food coloring & paintbrush
- Scrap of white card
- Colored pens
- Cocktail stick
- Glue
- 5½oz (150g) chocolate-covered honeycomb bars
- 12in (30cm) circular cake board (painted black)
- Chocolate stars
- Silver sugar sprinkles, stars, and balls

59

Step 1

To make the cake, preheat the oven to 320°F/160°C and grease the two tins. Beat the butter and sugar until light, then add in the eggs, one at a time, beating until combined. Add the vanilla extract and fold in the flour and baking powder. Divide the mixture between the tins and bake for 50–55 minutes. Remove from the oven and leave to cool before turning out.

Step 2

Score a circle in the middle of the flat part of both cakes, approximately 4in (10cm) in diameter. Scoop out both circles to a depth of around 2.5in (6cm). Now is the point to freeze the cakes if you want to make them in advance—cover in plastic wrap to prevent them from drying out.

Step 3

Make the buttercream frosting by beating the butter, confectioners' sugar, and vanilla extract together. Add the milk, a little at a time, until the buttercream frosting is a smooth, spreadable consistency. Add black gel food coloring to the mixture a little at a time, until you have a pale moon-gray color.

Step 4

Chop the honeycomb bars roughly into bite-size pieces, then add a sprinkling of edible glitter. Add a layer of buttercream frosting around the top of one of the cakes. Fill the scooped-out cavity with a heaped pile of honeycomb moon rocks. Scatter on silver balls, stars, and sprinkles. Place the other cake on top and press gently to seal

Step 5

Spread a layer of gray buttercream frosting around the whole cake. Roll out the gray ready-to-roll fondant icing to a thickness of ¼in (5mm), then cut out 8–10 circles and place them around the cake randomly to resemble craters. Add buttercream frosting around each one to build texture. Sprinkle a little edible silver glitter on the cake.

Step 6

To make the rocket, roll a grape-size piece of red fondant icing into a sausage shape. Form a point at one end and place it onto the cake. Cut three small fondant triangles to resemble the rocket legs and press onto the base. Paint the tip of the rocket, the legs, and a circular window using black gel food coloring.

Step 7

For the flag, cut a small rectangle of card and decorate with your child's name or a flag design. Glue the flag onto the cocktail stick and push it into the cake next to the rocket. For a finishing touch, use the handle of a teaspoon to make footprints in the surface of the moon.

If your cake tins aren't very sturdy you can place them into another circular cake tin to keep flat in the oven.

The sponge cakes can be made in advance and frozen—which saves time near to the party but also makes decorating the cakes easier.

TEMPLATES

Rocket Pencil Case (see page 40)
ENLARGE TO 200%

Rocket Toy
(see page 24)

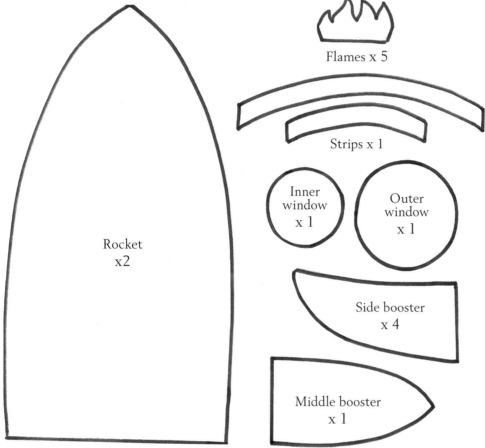

Flames x 5

Strips x 1

Inner window x 1

Outer window x 1

Rocket x2

Side booster x 4

Middle booster x 1

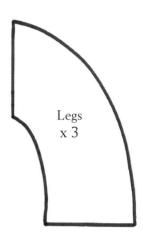

Legs x 3

ENLARGE TO 200%

Space Race Game
(see page 36)

PHOTOCOPY AT 100%

Alien Hand Puppet (see page 52)
ENLARGE TO 200%

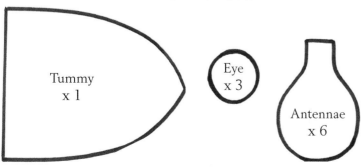

Tummy x 1

Eye x 3

Antennae x 6

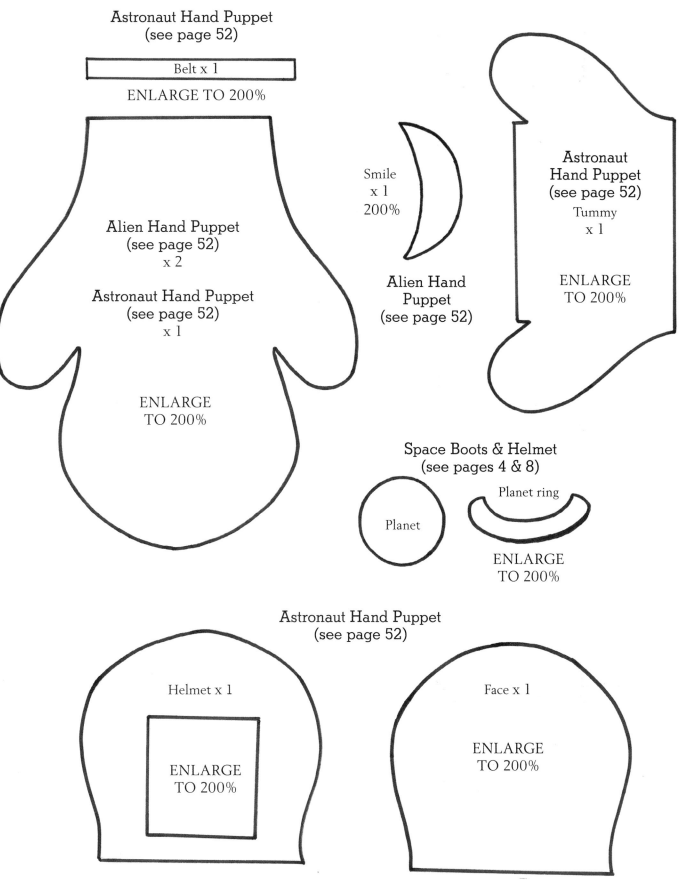

Astronaut Hand Puppet
(see page 52)

Belt x 1

ENLARGE TO 200%

Alien Hand Puppet
(see page 52)
x 2

Astronaut Hand Puppet
(see page 52)
x 1

ENLARGE
TO 200%

Smile
x 1
200%

Alien Hand
Puppet
(see page 52)

Astronaut
Hand Puppet
(see page 52)
Tummy
x 1

ENLARGE
TO 200%

Space Boots & Helmet
(see pages 4 & 8)

Planet

Planet ring

ENLARGE
TO 200%

Astronaut Hand Puppet
(see page 52)

Helmet x 1

ENLARGE
TO 200%

Face x 1

ENLARGE
TO 200%

Laura Minter and Tia Williams are two creative mums and good friends from Brighton, UK. *Little Button Diaries*, their award-winning blog, is filled with crafty things to do and make with your children. They have worked with major retailers including Hobbycraft, Cath Kidston, Paperchase, Mollie Makes and Laura Ashley. They spend their days running between each others' houses, with four kids and craft bags in tow.

Visit www.littlebuttondiaries. com, or come and say hello@ littlebuttondiaries.com

To place an order, or to request a catalog, contact: GMC Publications Ltd, Castle Place, 166 High Street, Lewes, East Sussex, BN7 1XU, United Kingdom. Tel: +44 (0)1273 488005

www.gmcbooks.com